a gift of love for:

_____

from: _____

Published by Sellers Publishing, Inc.
Text and illustrations copyright © 2012 Sandy Gingras

Sellers Publishing, Inc.
161 John Roberts Road, South Portland, Maine 04106
Visit our Web site: www.sellerspublishing.com
E-mail: rsp@rsvp.com

ISBN 13: 978-1-4162-0851-8

10 9 8 7 6 5 4 3 2

Printed and bound in China.

I Love you,

because...

by Sandy Gingras

SELLERS
PUBLISHING

When we love someone, we love to count the ways.

We love to say, "I love you, because of your sweet little nose and funny crooked toes..."

We love to enumerate the many varied things we notice and hold dear, the things that define our love and make it "ours." And we love to count how many ways loving another person has changed us and made our lives better too.

And once we start counting, we can't stop. There are so many reasons! "I love you, because, and because and because..." This is just a beginning.

I Love you,
because...
Around you, I can
be

my imperfect self

and my best self.

And you love me
just the same.

I Love you,
because...

I can Lean

on you

I Love you,
because...

you light my fire

I Love you,
because...

When I get all tangLed up,

you help me to

I love you,
because...

You tickle

my funny bone.

an adventure.

I love you,
because...
You believe in me.

I Love you,
because...
You understand
that a little kiss
can make a big
difference.

I Love you,
because...

I love you,
because...
When I'm with you,
I feel like I
can reach the stars.

I love you,
because...
you're honest.

You keep growing and changing

and making Life new.

you understand me.

I love you,
because...

I Love you,
because...

You are my sunshine
when the sky is
gray.

with every little thing
that you do.

I love you,
because...
You're warm

I love you
because...

We can be like kids
when we're together.

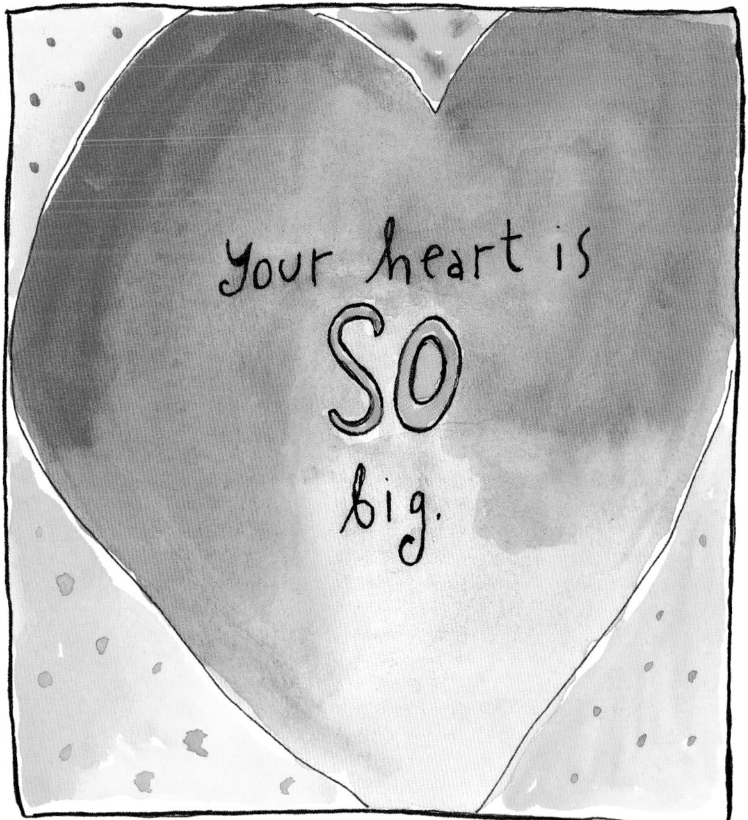
Your heart is
SO
big.

I love you,
because...
When I'm with you,
I feel like I'm home.

I Love you,
because...
you don't play
games

with my heart

I Love you,
because...

I Love you,
because...

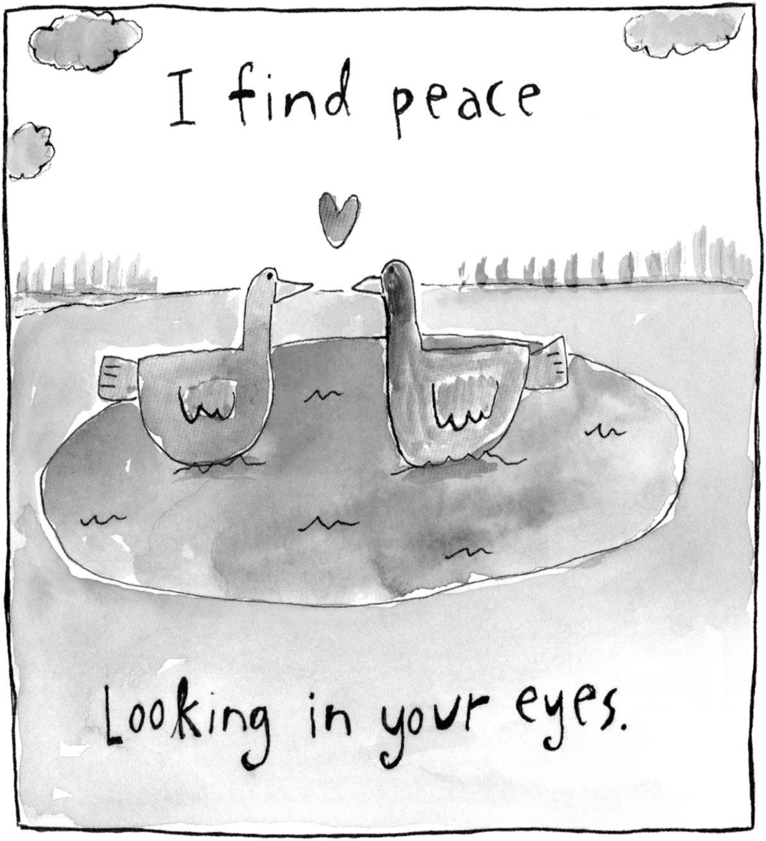
I find peace
Looking in your eyes.

I love you,
because...

When I'm around you,

I open up.

I love you,
because...
You light the
candles at dinnertime

and stir the night
with anticipation.

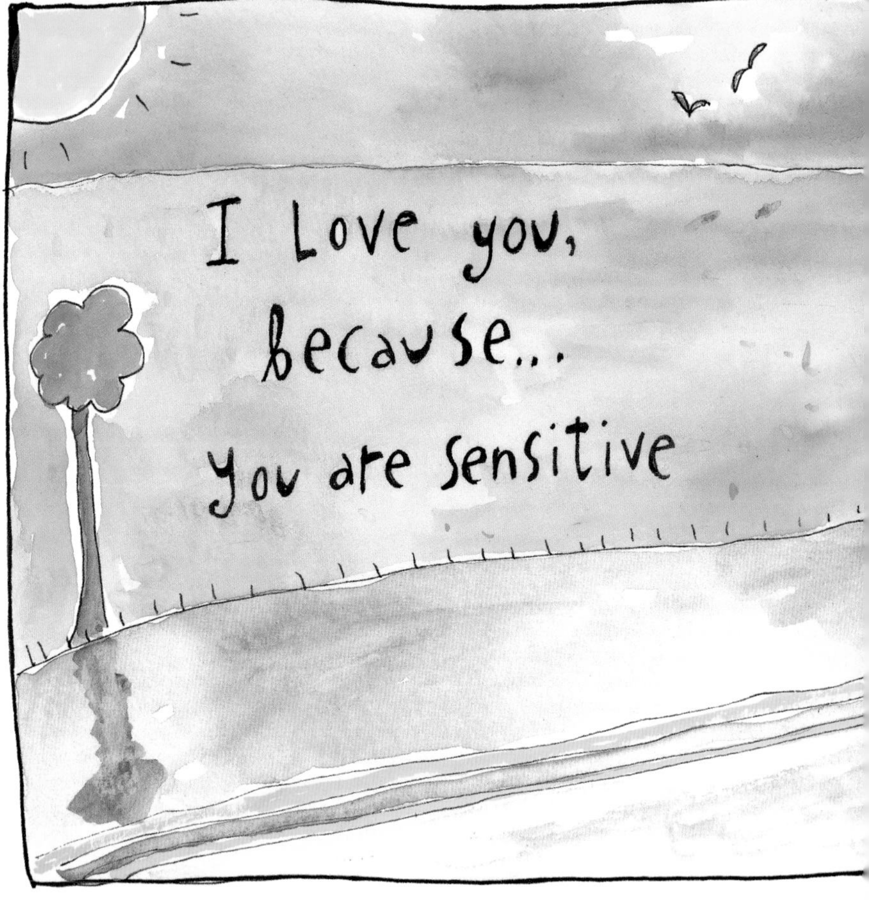
I Love you,
because...
you are sensitive

I Love you,
because...

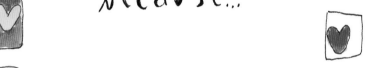

When you hear my voice,

I can hear you smile
over the phone.